THE KNIFE THROWER'S GIRL

The Knife Thrower's Girl

Naomi Mulvihill

WINNER OF THE 2022 WASHINGTON PRIZE

Andrea Carter Brown, Series Editor

THE WORD WORKS

Cover design: Susan Pearce
Cover Art: "Untitled." Rupert D. Turnbull, 1938,
oil on canvas, Smithsonian American Art Museum,
gift of Patricia and Phillip Frost
Author photograph: Jessie Auger

Excerpt from *A Breath of Life* by Clarice Lispector,
translated by Johnny Lorenz, copyright © 1987
by the Heirs of Clarice Lispector,
translation copyright © 2012 by Johnny Lorenz.
Reprinted by permission of New Directions Publishing Corp.

LCCN: 2022946618
ISBN: 978-1-944585-68-6

Acknowledgments

Grateful acknowledgement to the editors of the following publications where these poems first appeared:

Beloit Poetry Journal: "Dubbed, Staked Out, Overwritten—"

Cave Wall: "Waking"

Cimarron Review: "Life Science"

CutBank: "Invitation"

The Fiddlehead: "The Scuffle"

The Florida Review: "Sea of Crisis" and "Lake of Forgetting"

Georgetown Review: "Other Song/of Myself" (as "Love")

Green Mountains Review: "Annuals" and "Poetry"

Green Mountains Review Online: "Necessity"

Iron Horse Literary Review: "An Instant Before Impact" and "Order"

Kenyon Review Online: "In the Garden of Intelligence" (excerpt)

Michigan Quarterly Review: "Poly-, Ambi-"

New Orleans Review: "Ashes" as Web feature, "Cold War Couplets" (as "Cold War Ghazal"), "Pastoral" and "Step Inside"

New South: "Palmistry"

Passages North: "Cesium 137"

Salamander: "Gospel"

Unamuno Author Series Festival Anthology: "Necessity"

Verse Daily: "Poetry"

West Branch: "Timeshare"

Heartfelt thanks to Brian Henry and Factory Hollow Press where "Annuals," "Sea of Crisis," "Lake of Forgetting," "Dubbed, Staked Out, Overwritten—," "Poetry," "Necessity," "Other Song/of Myself," "An Instant Before Impact," "Sonia Says," "Poly-, Ambi-" and "Waking" appeared in *We All Might Be*, the 2022 Tomaž Šalamun Chapbook Prize Editor's Choice Selection.

Deepest gratitude to the Fine Arts Work Center in Provincetown, MA, and to Richard Blanco in Bethel, ME, for the gift of time. To The Word Works for believing in my manuscript and to Andrea Carter Brown and Nancy White for their wisdom, care and guidance in the final stages of bringing this book into being, I am profoundly indebted. As always, thanks to all my teachers who gave so much so freely.

Love and thanks to Duy Đoàn, Cate Marvin and Spencer Reece for their insight and support.

Contents

IV

V

"Come and see my home.
It's anyplace where nobody gives orders."
—Bessie Head

"I am in a certain hurry to feel everything."
—Clarice Lispector

I

Inside is a someone

Step Inside

1.
In the cellophane pages of an anatomical atlas, one
system overlays the last. Under a bone dome, the brain,
a scarred bride, drags her nervous train.

2.
Was it to purge herself of herself that my mother gave birth?
We were a body, composite—seven of us, stunted
and over-brimming—our own god.

3.
My sister sits on her hams in this dream I keep having.
Rigged with a bomb in her chest, set to detonate, she's
the instant, abscessed.

4.
Would she relent if she could? An ancient book
of the body gives us a figure—a knife in one hand,
his skin in the other. I want to hold her.

5.
Valverde de Amusco plagiarized flagrantly
from a work by Andreas Vesalius.
Later many of the remaining plates were credited
to Gaspar Becerra, an apprentice of Michelangelo's.

6.
As that flayed man crossed centuries, radiant
with a burden he couldn't dispose of, barely sixteen,
I pumped gas and sold cigarettes at the Sunoco.

7.
I must have thought my mother would rescue me
from my boss, a roguishly handsome mechanic who kept a .38
by the register. He had a habit
of running his hands under my shirt.

8.
Packed with black powder, the subcutaneous fuse
takes its signal by remote. Was the plagiarist merely lazy?
I ask my sister. I'm all hers—the heart's lop-sided knot,

9.
the incipient blast: Is it de Amusco's or Becerra's
or the flayed man's skin? *What makes us a single person,*
she says, *is our fear of being separated for good.*

An Instant Before Impact

Wasn't I a straight boy when I went home with him? Didn't he
tell me his mother had killed a child

one night on the coast road? He had a room above the garage.
One story below,

a small dark pool gathered under the car, tools leaned against the walls,
a mat of grass dried inside the mower.

I didn't understand the bed and bare rafters then or the window's three
            panes,
a triptych's parsed view—

marsh, still water, our faces and hands flattened and given back as glass.

Pocked with a few whitish stars, the sky riffled the tree-line, turning
and turning

the leaves' silvery undersides. From up there I could have watched us:
when he tried to make my body his,

when he moved through me like panic through a crowd,
we multiplied

into a jagged tangle of limbs and then thinned again
to a familiar symmetry.

I had wanted the room to become surf, but only a faint smell of surf
was there around the pain of form

crystallizing as I turned into myself,
a stunned girl.

Poly-, Ambi-

I'm writing a book where there's a blessing for each thing,
even Shredded Wheat, even an earthquake.

When I try to figure it out, silence snows me in.

On a song, there's a bird in the yard
that won't decide. Mocks them all—gull,

jay, car alarm. There's the man who leaps off a cliff

in a wingsuit and a mole that hunts the dunes
by seismic cues.

As fast as a path opens ahead, the sand collapses.

Tiny stranger, alien multitude—the only baby I ever made
came at the end

of the third month. Outside the first blades of grass

vent themselves along cracks in the asphalt.
Under a privet, violets condense

in the shadows' overlap. *Matter and its absence*,

the bird sings. Bless the unknowable. Bless the implausible.
Bless the ambivalent.

Invitation

A mallard bathes in meltwater at the pond's southern curve, his cautionary
orange feet, practical and rubbery as galoshes.

Beneath the pitted mother-of-pearl there must be a still place
waiting—under a latch-hole, a hundred kinds of blackness

and a flowering, somewhere, of gills. Tread lightly,
the mallard says, leaving a faint herringbone of prints in the snow.

My friend—a student of Buber, who fills her sideboard with receipts
and paper roses,

says she's not eating much these days by which she means everything
she does not eat lets her grow

empty enough to receive the world. I'm confused by violence against the self
in service of the spiritual, though I'm

given to violence myself. Exit the elevator at level 4
where patients wear regular clothes

and no window opens. In the ward's café, a woman named Roxanne
hatches her wedding plans. The whiskered attendant

will be maid of honor. Come. Everyone will be there. Mauve tabletops
conceal their bolted pedestals. A man paces inside

a set of eight linoleum squares. When my friend speaks to me
of an agony of narrowness I don't know

how to listen. I think instead of an animated film I've seen, every picture
made in sand, of a skater who as she turned became a fissure in the ice,
            into which

she vanished.

Necessity

When I worked in an orphanage a boy
came to harvest sugar cane in what
he'd worn to work the street at a beach resort.
His bunkmates picked up volcanic rock
I later learned geologists call scoria—a word
whose root gives us slag, drek
and excrement. At the field's edge,
they stoned him. I see his diminishing blue
still, the turbulence of his dress as he ran.
Out of jealousy or boredom they
also killed each other's adopted strays.
Then, I didn't know what it was to wake
in a woman's bed and enter the world
sure her touch must show on my skin.

Other Song
of Myself

To the one who's ingested an open safety pin, ribs, louver-like,
letting in the x-ray's blue evanescence, a softness
against which the metal tenses (call this a case of a sharpness

safer swallowed);
                        to the one covered in spurs and galls
for whom everything hurts—the curtain's white muslin, the muted tick
of steel down the hall;
                        to the shirtless girl whose heart

holds her body ransom and the boy who arches his back and laughs
when there's nothing to laugh at;
                                        in bewildered recognition of the throng
we are and are not supposed to be, the teeming

entirety;
        to wryneck and blindness of various kinds;

to every sort of fleshly extravagance, mix-and-match genital ensemble
bulge and twist: Welcome.

Parasitic Twin

Let me enter you.
Let me be the beast tethered in the dark stall of your body.
Let me sing to you in sleep, your own voice resting on the arc of mine.
Be my host. Hide me and keep me

or vanish into me when you are afraid
and watch from the projection room's high window
as our mother gives you a satin teddy with a snap at the crotch
and plods off to bed, leaving the door unlatched.

Curl up like a cat against my spine.
Enfold yourself in me. Let me be your blind.
From under my ribs, look out, slat-eyed.
I'll bear the extra leg, coyly undeveloped,

the rudimentary hand blooming at my waist like a corsage.
Promise me you'll go when I go—no sooner.
My ingrown edge, my black box,
be my song.

Sonia Says

So what if the better part of life is spent ugly and unaware,
eating alone in an unlit room?

My stepmom said, *I'm irked by your vulnerability, your
obtuseness*. Earlier that morning, I read

out loud from a book on garden pests
that described a kind of borer—something like a living tube of suet

whose sole defense is to recoil and vomit. Her comment
was unconsciously related, and somewhat true. She's all about

a plover feigning a broken wing to distract a fox from her eggs.
Why not make a beautiful display of desperation?

I'm about a blur of internal undulations. If a sexual spasm
could be encapsulated and let loose to roam the earth,

each wriggling movement a revolt against the knowable—
that might give you an idea of the borer's MO. Some days I see

no one. *Vulnerable. Obtuse.* I'll take it
a step further: *Don't look*

like a disaster bag (she wanted to say) *zipped around a victim.
Don't be something I can't name.*

Funny thing is they're all intimation—Would that be an eye?
That a leg? Unfuckable. And inside is a someone.

Palmistry

From a handbook my father left on a basement shelf,
we learned to kill
a man by shoving the delicate bones of his nose

into his brain. We'd pose like the pictures of the men
in the manual,
our deadly hands crossed by lines—one for head,

one for heart, one for life. I'd imagine bone shards
carving a path through
the infoldings and faults of a stranger's mind,

his hands with their heart, head, and life
lines, and the smaller ones
that run like back alleys webbed with shadows

and the stink of piss, towards little moments of intrigue,
chance encounters,
winning streaks—dropping away from my throat

where he had tightened them. And me?
I feel as if I'd slipped
under a veil into a sleeping child's skin.

Cold War Couplets

In a Mexican bar room, William Burroughs played William Tell on a lark.
His common law wife took the bullet through her temple.

Our neighbors braced for nuclear winter—a thousand cans in the
        fallout shelter.
Though we had no land, my father bought a mule.

Like Burroughs, my mother was partial to cats—to their sharkskin tongues
and alien grace, to the riddle they made of themselves. Father didn't
        love mules;

he loved the jack for fucking a mare on brazen impulse. Before
        albino swallows floated
over Chernobyl, we knew life was a walk on a rolling barrel.

While the radio rehearsed emergency alerts, my mother combed
and combed the black waste of her hair.

Cumulus bulge on the horizon, ampoules on the side table. What god
can claim an atomic child?

Calico Jane stroked her catnip mouse and dreamt of slipping manacles
on a lark. Honest John brayed, grinning and jaundiced, enshrined
        in his filth.

Pastoral

Under a private awning of thick branches
and thinner spurs, fused end to end with fruit,
the drops—pecked, cankered—turn to sacks
of vinegar. A family of social wasps
flickers yellow and black. Some funnel themselves
down a hole, some file out. All day it's
grind nectar out of flesh, it's listen to the larva
twitch. I hide at the canopy's filigreed edge.

My mother gathers wash. Absent,
a little havoc in one hand, she pairs the socks.
Mr. Riley, Mr. Davis, and Mr. Mount
are her real vocation. She dresses me in red velvet,
my sister in an old fashioned bonnet.
She folds us all seam to seam, cuff to cuff.
The grown-ups smile and speak in screams.

When I go to leave, she gives me an apple—
a ruffled calyx, ten pips, two in each waxy capsule,
two wooden tears huddled—and bends to unroll a bolt
of white cloth. Through a tumult of leaves,
I rise over a shrinking landscape. The sky
billows wide, a lax arc, then tightens as my mother
begins, with her free hand, to wind the fabric back.

The Knife Thrower's Girl

Because you will not come
into my grief, I will shape yours:

Before I could speak, she
spoke through me.

What she didn't know
I knew for her.

What she didn't fear
I feared for her.

I feared her.
She was the knife

thrower; I was his girl.
Also the reverse.

I pretended I died.
Then I pretended she died.

Because you will not,
I will—

every exchange,
a permutation of the first.

II

encLOSE

In the Garden of Intelligence

An early and well-known captive animal reserve, a precursor to a zoo, was created by Wen Wang, founder of the Zhou Dynasty in China (11th century, B.C.). He called this walled-in park the "Garden of Intelligence."

~

Lispector

Hen: animal I can
never understand—warm blooded
with no navel, inventor of the oval,
that shape that asks, Is the world
infinite?

~

Pizarnik

Hind quarters
half slunk, pacing

on the other side
of a name plate,

the wild dog
isn't.

~

Hikmet

I didn't know I loved bats—how they
hang by an ankle's stem. One hobbles along
a branch on the bone hooks of its thumbs.
I love its dissident biology—
black, well-oiled eyes it can live without,
wings that are webbed hands. All fur
and foreskin, private as the little thing
between the legs, it preens. It fans.

~

Levis

A suburban white girl with
the rosette pattern of a leopard tattooed
across one shoulder laughs softly
into her phone in front of my enclosure.
Bitch, you know I'd be murdered
to experience it, she says, gazing
vaguely past the ooze of traffic
to the First Baptist Church
and ALL CHECKS CASHED, her
body jonesing for what she calls
"reality," a word that might
rather be "snow globe," & lose everyone
who lifts and turns it to the charms
of its quaint, synthetic world.
Imposter, born in a gated community,
dosed with Vermifuge and Prozac,
I oblige my trainers. In me, she fails
to recognize her double,
another suburban white girl
wanting to be an animal.

~

Svevo

To every passing woman
the ass says, We've met.
Do you remember? You rode me
into Bethlehem.

~

Sappho

mine is the gland that suffuses
the room with a scent
that hardens into a resin

~

Baldessari

Outback
her hair in his harelip
Australia was admitted
except for Elmore

~

Larkin

When carrion's your business,
you piss on your hands

to sanitize them. Your
bald head you call

an exigence of cleanliness.
The condors lunch at 1:00.

~

Arbus

Nick and Marla loading Willie and Dandy for transport

Naming ceremony for baby giraffe, Binti

Chimpanzee playing Magic Piano on iPad

Woman in "not virgin but worth preserving" tee shirt

Silverback on life support

~

Lorde

How often do you have
to ask, "When a white woman
recites my poems, am I
trapped in my words in her?"

~

Smart

For I will consider the porcupine
who circles his whiskers, softly rigid, not quite grazing the wire grid
at the base of his den to achieve all feeling without touch;
Who limits his inroads to a perimeter, pounded out with fore paws
          and back,
Or cuts a diagonal by-pass to shorten the distance home;
Whose comings and goings derive a theorem
in which internal and external life are one;
Who dawdles at the water trough;
Who naps under an awning;

Who hones by grinding his incisors;
Who, struck by the impulse to multiply, tries to mount his mate;
Who, rebuffed when she erects a bulwark of spines, trundles
          undaunted on;
Who strikes sometimes a leisurely pose, lying on one side as he eats,
Or eats standing and fans his tail like a peacock in molt.
Last creature, or next to last, after an almighty sweep of destruction,
          his body is a thicket,
A burden of hollowness, a forest of affliction,
Homage to God.

~

Pizarnik

Jote, sos mi
infatigable vos.

~

Matta-Clark

encLOSE

~

"Box" Brown

not stars—

blackness held

at knifepoint

~

Mayakovsky

I turn my back
on this race of rats—naked,
all but blind, indifferent to pain;

hogs, hedge- and wart-,
for the camera, hamming;
birds whose heads don't fit
the bill; so many idle
piles of flesh, plying the crowds
with an eyebrow's
twitch, shackled to the hour
that fills the feed dish.

Time hails and hails me with a salvo
of petals! I won't be kenneled.
I'm the month from now
when we'll know something else.
I'm older than thought. The will of all
things wanders in me.
I'm the sound of angels
preening. Wake up, buttercup,
from your dreams
of vagabondage. We'll
sell mothballs and ruble vodka
from a kiosk on Nevsky Prospekt
and manitas de puerco
on Avenida Santos Degollado!
We'll hawk erotic comics
in sepia print! You'll be a figurine
of ancient terra cotta,
knocked-up and sobbing;
I'll be a 15th century woodcut
depicting a slaughter-of-
innocents scene. You'll be a coin-flip;

I'll be a shiv—all shorthand
for Won't you come with?

You hesitate.
Why?

Look what a lovely pen
and nice paper they've
given me to nest in!
Host to the vagrant:
Mendeleev's table,
laughter,

Josephine Baker,
Haight-Ashbury's Summer of Love,
the Volga Bulgarians,
snow,
I stoke the samovar
with unwritten manuscripts
of Asimov in these new tropics
of the North where all things converge.
Even god—lonely in robes
of lichen, licking his wounds,
and with a hind leg, peddling
the air—is here.
Call it a salon.

~

Popa Whitman Popa

Out of the blue womb of heaven
A shy and hidden bird is warbling a song.
We mock the song.

~

Paglen

yak
DARPA
dik-dik
oryx
lynx

~

Mother Goose

foam of cud
on the lower lip
line of drool
body built
to house
a vacant look

            . . .

not the Mobius strip
asleep in the bowl
of my lap but one
unbundling a skein
of gut

            . . .

see the cow
see the cat
see the silo
where my boy
drowned
in gold oh

~

Ovid

Mapped be your genes;
weighed, your meals and excreta;
In exchange for safety, may every hour
of every day be live-streamed—
your empty gaze pixilated, genitals
paraded, flesh made data.
May your unsatisfied sex drive

be eclipsed only by an even greater desire
to die. Visitor, may you exist entirely
without mystery. May you be
obliterated by visibility.

~

Mayakovsky

Let me be your Vlad
in full flower, your wolf-boy
whose skin has grown
over his collar.
No, you say! Then I'll lodge
like a stowaway
bullet in your heart.
I—unaccountable
happening—avalanche
and its aftermath, who can
make a field of poppies bloom
through a buttonhole, turn
like a falling leaf in your wake.

Love, if you won't have me,
grant me one wish. Let me
lose—fair and square—
even longing.

I'll press an ear to my heart
and be lulled
by the ruddy murmur
of blood filling my lungs.

Remember, you've snubbed me
more than once, like my Mauser,
luck would have it. And as luck
would have it, the more you smite
me, Kitty, the more I'm smitten.
But don't be fooled.
They've swapped out
for in and built around you
a brilliant mise-en-scène.
No detail—the vandal named Arlo,
his skull haloed in gold curls, carving
a one-word epic into the plexiglass
that separates us; the steel
and epoxy trees, and escarpment
of poured concrete—is amiss.

In a jump cut of years,
Morris, Anglin and Anglin will
synchronize swim the bay of Alcatraz.
No one will ever discover them.
The only thing left to do is
subtract yourself from the set.

~

Joplin

She lifts her tail to spray
the bamboo and licks the snow.
The sound she makes isn't a roar.
If you closed your mouth while shouting,
if you stuffed a rag down your own
throat or rose to stand and fell
in the same damn motion—

~

G-d

Open-mouthed, unhinge yourself. Slough off your skin.
Let the tip of your tail slip—your body, your one

utterance—through the ghost of your throat to return
to the wordless beginning.

~

Sor Juana

Watch me become what's not
silence and not said.

~

Lorde

Poet, what does it mean
to earn your keep?

III

closer, closer, more remote—

Poetry

Child of a lighthouse keeper and a firewatch,

conceived in a wordless encounter

at a rest stop—

1 part flywheel, 8 parts restraint—

luminous with near-disaster,

says, Don't try to mirror this

world of nothing-is-as-it-seems.

Set down no word. Says, by means

of a searching pause

I mistake for an intimate nod,

Step inside the caution tape.

Timeshare

By the pool where the stink of chlorine
competes with the stink of cats,

the swing set snipes all day
at the horseshoe pit. A small tangle

of girls with chipped, press-on nails
divvies up a vial of x.

The sky's calamine, a zincky-ferrous pink,
masks a stinging

swarm. *Stay*, says the fescue's pale frill,
Keep quiet. See things. A starling

scores a daub of beef
in the Arby's parking lot. On a tuft

of clover, resisting the wind pianissimo,
a weevil effs its mate.

Closer, closer, more remote—
birth date, blood type, sub-umbilical

factors of risk, now into my bones
where hourly

billions of cells unplug themselves,
atom by atom, matter gives spirit

the slip. A booklouse doctors the files.
Five crows mouth off

to the ozone's widening hole. A gull
snuffs a whelk. No one stalks

the nocturnal rove beetle,
not over-beautiful,

that gaits along like me, but multiplied
—right foreleg in time with left

middle and right back—
as it combs the wrack for fleas.

Cesium 137

A man means to make a ring for his wife.

For you, I mean to make a poem.

The man lives on the periphery of a distant city.

We live around the corner from a methadone clinic on a charmless street.
Realtors call it a neighborhood "in transition."

At home in a scrapyard's oxides, its smell of motor oil and hemoglobin,
the man is a purveyor of junk and treasure.

We are trying to salvage ourselves.

A delicate, awful matter, someone is apt to get hurt.

Driven by *What's in there?* and *What can be redeemed?* a few employees
extract a cylinder from a piece of abandoned medical machinery. They
puncture the capsule with simple tools.

My life has been a confused and elaborate effort to outsmart the ordinary

An ectoplasmic blue. The man takes it from the workshop into the bedroom.

One night, I say, "We'll die without ever really knowing each other"
—a perpetual loneliness I recklessly call "boredom."

Novelty proffers itself. The future glows through the seams
in the top dresser drawer.

Of the two of us, I am the more destructive.

You launch yourself at tedium by putting your hands on things, tending the ro
Suffering buds up, reciprocated with blossoms

of suffering. Will one of them go before he learns how to work his medium? Or will they both, of overexposure? The red talc gathers

fingerprints. Your hand, in sleep, reaches. Rotating a wrist, you open your fist—a magician performing a dove trick. Longing turns a body

into a clock. I am afraid. This is how love looks.

Now

for Fred

Some part of you dutifully folds
and misfolds proteins
until in your own body
you are entangled. Led out
of the I by small irregular steps,
you've taken up painting
in the style of van Eyck.
I can imagine no worse idea
or more perfect—*How?*
I ask, knowing how one hand
holds the other's clamor—
a more psychedelic van Eyck:
dreamy, haphazard,
forecasting Cabeza de Vaca
and his eccentric dead
reckoning, lost in the scrub
of the fourth horseman's beard
in the Altar of Ghent,
as he hummed along
with Canned Heat.

At odds with "at the mercy of,"
in the service of "at full tilt,"
a brain works roundabout.
Roundabout, a lunge
incites your right arm to rise,
dyskinetic, casting away
a hand, which comes to rest
near your throat with a touch
that startles your torso, as if
tapped by a stranger on the back.
Back up the hand goes,
circling—condensing, refining
a motion through a set of

consciously imposed limits
to become a gesture, tender,
familiar, a slight pressure
between thumb and index
finger on the lower and upper
rim of your glasses, delicate
adjustment that by millimeters
brings us immeasurably closer—
certitude arrived at by dint
of palsy. *See me I am sad*
and beautiful, your body says,
retreating I approach open
your eye let me in.

The Chance Art of Pigeons

for John Cage and Zhang Huan

Does it happen like this: High tide, after dark
a Vegasy sound? They lift off, shuffling
and reshuffling themselves
into an organized flock or sometimes
in their resistless rise and turn, snow
echoes snow and they sift
onto the shingled roofs
of shops. I've seen how they leave
tracks over tracks over tracks
on a shrinking patch of shore—
a hallucinatory saturation of space
like a serial self-portrait in which calligraphers
have written the names of ancestors
and traditional Chinese text on an artist's face,
inking in characters until the man is blotted out
or inscribed, perhaps.

Do the pigeons go and land again
to huddle, each one balled against the cold
and rising tide? Is there an absolute center—
a hot spot—as they mass? In the dunes I've
thought of recording the sound
of beachgrass, a blade's regular sweep
in a chance breeze as it traces a circle
around itself. A blur of toe prints as sound
is worth eleven radios, and suppose I saw
the pigeons at night in plain view? I wouldn't
know what they were up to. When people
kiss you can't know what, if anything, the kiss
may hide or reveal.

On Landmarks

According to the book
on my lap, a *toot* is a hill
suitable for observation. A *pap*
is a mountain or hill whose shape
is thought to resemble a woman's
breast. I barely know my brother.
At thirty-six, he knows
many things. If you ask
him about *Charlotte's Web*,
which he's mastered in braille,
he will tell you that Charlotte's job
is to be a spider and Wilbur's
is to be a pig. Even E.B. White
did not fully understand this.
My brother's never seen himself,
and doesn't read anything
into a landscape.

Dubbed, Staked Out, Overwritten—

from the Atlas bone that holds
up my head to my Achilles tendon;
every hemisphere, groove,
fissure, plate, ridge and basin;
from Broca's area in the frontal lobe
that controls my ability to say "tubes,"
Eustachian or Fallopian, to each tract,
notch, root, bend, inlet, loop,
crevice and recess; from the spiral
valves of Heister, affiliated somehow
with bile, to my bundle of His,
pores of Kohn and canal of Nuck
just beyond the vestibule
of my vulva—I've been occupied
by centuries of men. My body
is an index of them.

Order

Between nap and nape is napalm,
between the flutter of eyelids and back
of the neck, a wall of gelatinous flame.

Jowl hangs above joy, lot beneath lost.
Where mess goes, message follows. A dog,
hit by a car, extrudes its own intestines
as it leaps around children on a seesaw.
See how delight rides shotgun with dread.

Cud lives in cuddle and tusk sits pointedly
under tush. HIV and hive collapse
and disappear, letter by letter, reeled
back to an aspirate. Mercury leaches

into mercy, leaving us twice blessed
by tunnel vision and numbness downstream.

Jubilee

With the skeletal notation of bonds, double
bonds, hexagons—complete and unhinged,
cultivation begins.

Spokes reach like half-thoughts. A torn honeycomb
confected from the Periodic Table's spare abecedary
lies

beneath an elegant chemical index—methyl
viologen, halosulfuron, diazinon—
fronted, in turn,

by the trade names' tongue-in-cheek:
Flint, Twist, Bravo,
Roundup, Tritex-Extra,

Sandea, Paraquat, Adios Bait,
invisibly applied by an undocumented hand,
injected

into the irrigation drip line, broadcast
from the back of a tractor or, more intimately,
a polyethylene tank worn as a knapsack.

The Poet & the Astronaut

ARMSTRONG: Where's the freaking earth?
Where the hell is the horizon
with the world coming over it?
ÉLUARD: The earth is blue
like an orange. We have dreamt
within us Space
for the greatest silence.
Neil, the honeycomb
of strength is stuffed with filth.

Carry On

for Roger

A cowbird in the paper birch makes a sound in its throat
of pebbles dropped in water like Aesop's crow
raising liquid in a pitcher—plot driven by thirst,
resolved not by cunning but plodding labor.
The Dutch, they say, shut idle prisoners
in a cell where a sluice opened to let terror inch up.
Drown? Bail yourself out? You choose.
When I visit him, an ex-professor tells me he doesn't know
who I am. Plaque of Alzheimer's filling his mind, he
says, Shitcan the connectives. No time. Sit your ass
at the desk. Discipline's a writer's moral
imperative—advice I will surely forget. A more likely story
would have the crow surrounded by stones not too large
to lift, but too large to fit the vessel.

The Road Is Better

than the inn or so someone said:
the landscape up close, convulsive spikes
and discharges of pre-fab concrete
and abandoned cars impounded
by the state. A set of rails veers
off like an arm, mid-gesture—*What do I*
know? What do I care? Against the fence
pickets' staccato, sumac and burdock
go from a strobe to a blur. A few
seconds' lapse and the scenery—split-
levels, colonials—recomposes itself
into a sane wheel of pastels the color
of pills and glides, sedate,
detached: *I cannot love*

anyone. Jeff didn't wire the money
his father gave him. The bills for his stillborn
son's burial said IN GOD WE TRUST.
He flew to Acapulco. He spent
the week on the balcony trying to decode
Reforma and *Proceso.* He studied the beach
dogs—a melee of licks, thrusts
and, tails high, all-trot-off.
Mornings, he wandered.

Let it come to him—a fistful of bees
milling the fountain's dry spout;
a knife in a butcher's stall, deftly
separating membrane from meat.
Angling and receding, the blade
dipped—fly in milk, oar in fog—
under the film. At one corner
of the plaza, kids ran
a stick over an empty bleach bottle
to make a corrugated sort of sound.
The smallest of them wiggled her hips

for coins. Jeff lowered his eyes
to avoid other eyes and the names
of things. Fissures in the sidewalk
branched, neuron-like. A pattern
of mesh suggested chain-link.
Navigating by cracks and shadows,
he tried not to look more than a few yards
ahead. A vein of magnetic tape
from a cassette lead him down
an unpaved street. He came across
the pit of an unfamiliar fruit. It was hard
underfoot, and woolly and kept a secret

he sensed he understood. The trail
narrowed. The grade changed.
At a cliff, the path turned
to air: *Onward, pendejo, or*
relive each step. Below him, a procession
of whitecaps pressed in. He cut left
through the yard of a house,
half-built. A few dresses on a line
writhed like netted fish.

Watching a car chase, badly spliced,
in a movie on the express bus
to Chilpancingo, sandwiched
between a scene of speed
on video and the mental picture he'd
made of himself—window seat, row
six—gunning it down the viaduct,
he felt the baby's death
transmuted into something giddy,
distant, not his. He woke up
on a loading dock in someone else's shoes,
and they fit. If he was wearing slip-ons,

who was wearing his high tops?
A stranger—a smoke and a girl
shared between them?

An exposed cable dangled from
a light sconce in the hotel foyer.
Jeff took a seat on the patio
next to a decorative urn. The pack
mostly slept in depressions
under lounge chairs where tourists
would have dozed or read. They
wouldn't be petted. A pug
averted its gaze and cowered
in a trough between two palms.
One missing tufts of fur from mange
or burns rhythmically lapped a paw.
A shepherd slung a leg over
a buddy's rump and, just as quickly,
uncoupled. When a vendor struck
a match and dropped a lump of fat
on the griddle, their ears shifted

parabolically. The sea's smack and fizz
darkened the sand. Made somehow
of molecules, shaped out of and into slosh,
the waves—near, almost vertical,
gained height, leaned and overreached
themselves. An invisible force
went shoreward. The water rolled back
to its starting place. Parallel, the dogs
rose and loped in rough unison,
curving, purposeful. The catch
had come in.

At the end of the line, katydids
chafe and wind—frantic
and never coming to the point.
A redhead, boarding, waves
good-bye and hands a lit cigarette
to her mother, who's smoking another.

Jeff said, If I stole it was because I
couldn't stand the stillness. I said, No
shame in that. It's about what flashes
by: "tree" stenciled on the bucket
of an arborist's truck, an American
flag with one yellow stripe, the accordion
of green that sloughs off either side

of the train. We stop at the registry
of motor vehicles. We stop at St. Francis
rehab. We sit together in our isolette.
When the doors open, some of us
stand up abruptly. From the tunnel,
I walk to that pond where a man
plays an instrument with two strings.
His bow arm, draped
in a gray sleeve whose cuff
covers half of his hand,
acts injured or the music enacts some
grief. *I have lied. I have believed
my lies.*

If I Have One Regret—Send a Photo
So I Know How You Look—It's Not Having
Your Mother Committed

1.
What Could Be Worse Than Finding Them Dead?

Stand back, one of them says,
We are lepers. It must have been before
Balthazar mistook Ben-Hur for Jesus
but after the galley slave sequence
in which Heston unchains his mates,
floats on debris with an adversary
he's saved then hesitates, contrapposto,
above the hatch of the enemy ship
—our cat on the sill, twitching
its tail habitually—that my father
gathered us for what he called
a "ceremonial child beating."
Stripped to the skin, we
played along as extras.

2.
Ashes

He wanted his scattered
on the Outer Banks, where
I wandered one summer
past him naked in bed
with a woman, the two of them
sunburnt except for cutouts
of swim trunks and bikini,
the curtains' inebriated sway,
a barely audible abrading.
You had to walk through
the bedroom to get to

the bathroom where
there was a mirror and cool
water. It was 1973
at a conference he'd convened
in a house on stilts. My father
introduced my sister and me
to his following as "the slaves."
The hitchhiker hired
to man the kitchen
would be our master.

3.
Afterword

Something has drawn me out of my body—
that tail-chasing stray I called home.
We were recklessly devoted, sallying

onto private lawns, content to meet
the world at its crotch. We thought
rot and out of rot—everything

but this. You there, with the birthmark
like a smile, hidden in a fold of flesh, the one
I can't go on without, *Can you hear me?*

Won't you help? I'm caught in a loop.
I am shouting, and you are enclosed
in a to-fro of your own, considering the habit

of the elm, comfortably immersed
in its shadows. Listen, I'm assailed, as always,
by the same insatiable cravings, a mantra

of no *ne plus ultra*, my trove of failings,
the same conceptual gaps: algebra,
trans-national debt, the bird's-eye view

of almost anything. Even grief.
Even now, unable to make a sound,
I want you to think of me

as a loveable fuck-up
to cast myself a future
excuse for pain I have yet to inflict.

IV

is surrender the animal—

Primes

2
horsey puzzle me
me pen
pen me?

3
in a room alone
able to taste
the apple
from the inside

5
why did Milly go blind will you
be mad if I cut off my braids if I don't look
like a lion will I still make pawprints
in the mud are there babies
in hell remember my hand
with the fish hook in it how do you know
if someone's a stranger could a giant
water bug suck out my insides
when I grow up I want to be a moth
that pops like that in the lamp

7
At the gas station, gumballs are money in games of Tunk.

Dick and *Jane*, *Bob and Carol and Ted and Alice* are names to know.

The colors are primary and smeared with Lubriko.

When they say hog opera, they mean stockyard.

We ran toward the wreck because it was a carnival truck.

We made up our own game with four decks and no rules.

It's called *Cheat the Deal*; if you win fair and square, you lose.

11
When I was a boy,
my coach said to me, *Button it*
up, Mulvihill, or you'll be
fielding your own balls.
I thought in advance of time
to Pyotr Pavlensky, who
in protest of passivity will nail his
to the cobbles of Red Square,
for safekeeping, I'll send mine.

13
What's in a dirty virgin martini?

17
Deep from the pulp of the classifieds,
my sister asks: *Would you rather
be a Buick Electra or a Buick Caballero?*
question that opens onto an empty stretch
of road—a flaming rollover—in which
I recognize myself and drive on.

19
Sugar, my father says, I have something to ask of you. Sure, Dad,
I say, unwrapping a piece of gum, beginning to chew. It's your
mother. I don't know if you've noticed. She's not been herself.
We met with a specialist—early onset, but more virulent than
usual. She's already somewhat delusional. The hydrangeas
wave their blue crinoline. A sparrow pecks at a cigarette end.
Listen, he says, I can't see her through it. I know this sounds
crazy. The course of our lives has changed for good. I don't have
the stones to take care of her or the stones to undo her. Maybe
you can help her to the other side. I'll take some pills and
leave a confession for your alibi. Don't answer now, he says, I
think it's airtight. Dad, I say, but this is a lot to take in. Home
again, I see my mother's hair is flat on one side, overblown
on the other. She's bruised her wrist. Raising her gimlet, she
smiles, Hi, sweetheart, and slides a finger between the slats
of the venetian blinds. Is Daddy still out? I nod. Through the
gap, she surveils the sidewalk, the neighbor's garage, and
then angles herself uncomfortably to scan the cul-de-sac. A
branch scrapes across the carport roof. Good Christ! she says,
standing suddenly wild-eyed, upright. I'm afraid your father's
developed something of a gambling habit. He's pissed away
all of our savings. I rest my hands on the edge of the beige
davenport. Honey, she says, if we let him, he'll ruin us.

23
Condemned to the beasts
and by four angels carried
eastward, swimming drunk
in the dark and someone's
untethered the raft
where we'll never get,
a really bad trip
we can't regret—

29
Surfacing, we circle, emitting
at intervals an emerald
phosphorescent mm-hmm,
you-bet, da dit—third language
da da over which, splendidly,
no one has command.
The pitch of our signals
ratchets up until we
reach affirmative torque
and burst. Thoroughly
ransacked, rent to shreds,
to tiny anonymous pieces
that could be taken for tissue
of any living species, aleph-ish,
protoplasmic, we sink
to remake ourselves, as if
creation was saying: None of that
I'll be Jonnie to your Dollie; Why not
each a legion, eyeless and wingless
with unsettling behavior,
unsettled, unascertainable, apt
to explode whenever you
float amorously past.

31
In the rose's off-white volumes
is a poem that speaks to an element—
hypothetical—waiting to be born
of a cataclysmic event.

37
Alongside the crowd
a latecomer
stares off
into a drift
of unconstellated stars.
An oarboat circles.
Far from the murmur
of voices, a slow spiral
reshapes the lake.

41
can't touch bottom
&
can't climb out

43
Life is most possible in places named
Shell Pile, Old Rag and Huerfano,
populated only by loose ends, marl
and the small unclaimed bones of orphans,
though of course it is painful. No one speaks
the words PNUTS PORK on the sign
in the general store. In the absent marsh,
in a motion mimed by the rockweed,
a merganser drags one wing. An aftershock
hurls your shadow around a corner,
and mine, dead out ahead.

47
cereal into bowl: D-7 and D#-7, vivace, staccato with simultaneous
single, clear breath blown through flute. 2 seconds, sudden
start, trailing off. In the wait for your next round of pills, an
orange telegraphs the coordinates of every vessel
ever in distress.

spoon against bowl: F#-6—One note, we are (glockenspiel
slightly dampened w/ handkerchief) implausible,
an emergency.

glass breaking (point of impact): fingers begin on E-7, F-7, and
F#-7 keys & sweep upward to end at G-7, G#-7 and A-7 in a loud
and sudden ploy to distinguish self from not-self—fading.

child laughing at bus stop: Quick clear breath on flute (1/2
second) that ends on G-7, F#-7, E-7, D-7, played by piccolo
trumpet, staccato allegro growing fainter along with the colors
of lunchboxes, backpacks and bodies.

bird cleaning beak on aluminum gutter: Super guiro: Tee-Tee
rest. Though she's dead, your grandmother's still sharpening
her boning knife. Tee-Tee rest, Tee-Tee rest in peace.

53
how can I keep you strange
and keep you who's speaking can I
be trapped if there's no place
I'd rather be why does that animal
seem happy in its cage oh unknown my one
and only my beloved can you find my way
if I'm my sole audience does that make me a self-
operative or an auto-anthropologist
who will pronounce my sentence
on the terrible day will it happen
to not happen what's the balm
for the raw spot that's also a callous
is surrender the animal

59
ART AS BLOOD SPORT
BLOOD SPORT AS ART

61
Writing is a dance called Want.

Watch the moths at an incandescent lamp
as they charge the lumens.

The blood of bulls courses through them.

Where is Manolete, tricked out
in his *traje de luces*?

In Linares he said, *I can't feel anything*
in my left leg.

The moths slam their bodies in a dance

called Inside and Out Alike, Be a Sheet of Ice

Ablaze. *I can't feel anything in my other leg*,
Manolete said.

Are my eyes open?

Drumming their wings, they fling

themselves into the light. I like best
the ones with no need

even for a mouth: This is what feeds them.

67
I hear the nickering
of the blind mare
that lives behind
my eyes, and hum
Komm, süsser Tod
to her as I approach,
saying, "It's me,
I'm almost there."

71
Past any chance of selling ourselves
for scrap value, plasma and spare parts,
we ride along ahead of the sound
of our siren, thinking back
to the spring thaw's debacle—
our ship covered in brine
flowers and frost roses
that first voyage out,
& how we found happiness
depressing next to the Neva
with Ernesto, his mother's exile
long and white like a smock
of the incurable, something we
wanted impossibly
to try on for size and take off.

73

"What's in the basket?" the little iron man asks. Instead of apples, the first suitor lies and says, "Frog legs," and when he gets to the castle with a basket of frog legs, the king sends him packing.

"Hog bristles," the second suitor says in reply to the little man, afraid he'll be outwitted by someone so small and oddly ironclad. In the audience of the king, he uncovers the fruit of his guile—

apple is to hog bristle

The last suitor, the fool, answers "Apples," makes his way to the castle and saves his future bride who would die if it weren't for—

When your medicine cabinet becomes a medicine cabinet— private slum of amber plastic, white labels and white caps, not a catchall for ear plugs, teething rings, spare buttons, and ChapStick—that's when it happens: A rooster looks at you, cock-eyed. A duck ducks its head. A crane, by God, cranes its neck. A flounder, that simpleton, flounders on the seabed, seabed, seabed—

apple is to apple

79

Iced or smoked?
Plain or glazed?
Pit or stone?
Is who I am not
knowing who I am?
Am I the voice
I haven't met?

83
To this quintet
of sills, the *tic tic*
of the hanging
fixture and that runner
whose hypoxic blue
cuts a slow swath
down the center
of the table,
it's all the same.

89
You've landed a part in this magic
show. If the hat's a hole, would
that make my soul the rabbit?

97
Black from this distance, every bird—
every tree, black—
the inner song in all things—
and every apple.
We'll float home, each
our own craft.

V

I worry you'll end…

Life Science

The plot is full of the heads' noiseless forming,
the silent press. Glaucous blue, lenticular,

they thicken. Sunday morning:
a church bell, doves bathing

in grit. Off-white moths agitate the air.
They cluster and stray.

Next door no one moves. After noon,
he'll come down, affably disheveled.

She'll wear the housedress with long sleeves,
pins in her hair, her cleavage covered.

Shouting at the dogs, *Shut up you sons of bitches*,
he'll laugh and tend a pile of burning brush.

Bald, webbed with veins, the cabbages
muscle their way back into the frame. This one's

a gouty knee; this one's a brain swelling
against its case. Touch this one with a blade

and it herniates. I'm on the porch in red
shorts learning what I can from two saw flies

courting in a nail hole. When the wind
shifts, we'll drift in a squall of ash.

Sea of Crisis

A steamer burned and capsized one October,
setting loose its cargo

of apples and people—material for a parable.

One November, a mongrel
named Laika, launched on an elliptical orbit,

circled my parents

before they were my parents. Dead
only a few hours into her journey,

she spun weightless, an idea

realized. Someone said, *If a dog, then
a man*, so we had men

in a quarter million mile thrall

snapping photos of their own planet
with Hasselblads. They read

Genesis televised. The whole world

was aboard. My parents, by now, had waded
six years in. Off air, the astronauts

horse-traded bacon squares and beef bites

laughingly but something was different.
One said, *Back where the earth used to be*,

and the words filled

with epigraphic reverb. Apples and people—
what I know grows infinitesimal

in my dory. I row facing land, my back to

where I'm going. Of Laika, we know
hardly anything at all.
Part terrier, part husky, life in a sequence

of smaller and smaller cages
prepared her for outer space.

Lake of Forgetting

From the East, a shadow—leisurely,
untroubled—pours toward her.
I hold my mother from behind; hitch
her pants; lace belt through loops,
prong through notch, tongue through band.
She says, *I worry you'll end up childless*
like I have. Or trapped, she begins
to cry: we've missed an armhole. She
shows no recognition of me.
We fold and unfold our hands,
fan them in a chorus no one is sure of,
spoon the fruit the neighbors
can and call ambrosia.

The Scuffle

March is nesting season. Between barbs,
the last of the berries coagulate.
A female cardinal, dainty in a reptilian way—
her scaled legs, her overlapping feathers arrayed
scale-like—has stationed herself near
the picture window. Since morning—she rests
only to catch her breath—she's been attacking
her reflection. Beneath her obsidian eye,
what moves? What does she think?
She looks tired. Her buff brown outfit's
smeared with rouge. She flies at herself,
claws the glass. When she carried me, what
was it my mother thought? The cardinal
launches herself again against her double—
a half-dead eye, an aposematic orange beak.
When I was pregnant I thought, how
can I save this child from myself?

Annuals

Late September blossoms turn
themselves inside out in a crisis of light.

I am beginning to know
their built-in mobility, a stillness
in which they convulse.

Buttons, all pent up. Sticky ones
waver next to ones covered with gold
dust. The air scintillates

with bees; the ground, with ants.
A vee of geese moves loudly
southward. And I want to leave

myself in order to see. I want
the rose's self-perpetuating red

to transfuse the garden pint by pint.

Gospel

Rosie, who's dying of malabsorption,
yaps on the front porch. A walking ossuary,
she treads the matchboards and waits
for the Witnesses—two young women
who must smell faintly, I think, of fried food
or red rubber balls or mud. Rosie loves them
as she loves pork rinds, fetch, and puddles
and, because I'm promiscuous
in matters of faith, so do I. Any position
seems plausible. On days like this, we
bask in the late autumn sun and let the missionaries
limber us up with biblical small talk. Soon they'll
ask me about the afterlife. When I say
I don't feel the need for it, Rosie
will agree because we're a woman
and a dog of one mind. The blonde
in the pilled navy skirt will drop her voice
an octave, and almost whisper, "Even with all
the suffering?" Out of place in an immaculate sky,
a single cloud—a scoured spot
where the material has worn through—
will oversee our silence. They'll never
return and Rosie will die. I'll bury her red ball
with the handful of ash she's become.

Outside Tonopah, Arizona

Pigtail of vine on this end, blossom spot
on that; inside, red
satin. Somewhere a body sobs for it.

~

Steal me to eat in secret!
one in the field ventures against
a silent tightening of rinds.

~

Fruit of mutual pact—
I ravage you, you ravage me
back and it never grows old
and we're never used up.

~

To net what happens by
or net nothing

and ripen? An orb spider
and a melon
across a furrow

feel the draw
of self-through-other.

~

The ritual of execution is rewarded
with the counter-ritual of a last supper.
Two slices, ice cold. A mouth's live warmth.

~

When flesh and color fade, sweetness
will begin again
to seek its oblong incarnation.

Dress and Stuff Your Pig

Malinda Russell left us
instructions for how to let things speak
for themselves in the form of a cookbook
filled with cream cakes, icing
and silence, published in 1866
in Paw Paw, Michigan,
where she settled, having fled
what she called Tennessee *guerrillas*—
a mob of marauding white men—
who took her life savings, and promised
to take her life if she exposed them.

A calm surrounds her order.
Fried Rusk. Muffins.
Pickled Plums. Onion Custard.
This free woman, who made her way
alone with a son, wrote volumes
—*one pint new milk, blood warm*—
in a phrase. In the book of 39 pages,
there are five different recipes
called Cookies. The first is a list
of four ingredients without
a single directive.

Malinda Russell left us
with many questions, such as
Why does this manual resist
the use of imperatives?
Is what's unspoken common
kitchen knowledge or common knowledge
around the norms of race?
And could she know how the rare
imperative she did deploy
would resonate in the same crisis
one hundred fifty-four years on today?

Yes—Not at All

Where is it we keep
the scissors? Watch
that saucer under
the cabinet. I've been
feeding an orphan
opossum, a kitten really,
of a thing.

Hard to believe
how much rubbish
a flower makes.
Ox-eyes off-gas
dander. Lilies
stink like bedwetters—

I love them only a little less
than I love you
and your sisters, lost
to some idea of the mother
you pined for—it's safe
to say Nature

doesn't care.
And here they are!
Ingenious, these, that
cry out, Oh, if only

fingers were sabers!
And what of the tale
with the table
set for two, two beds
turned down and two
daggers waiting?

Does a scissors
prefigure—
The hip of the rose,
would that be the ovary?
—the cut? I'm their
instrument.
If I'm life's outpouring, you're
my outpouring. Don't forget

I gave you form. Dread
is the perfect mind-body blend,
don't you think? Remember
when you—no, I—
had that prolapse and everything
on the inside began to work

its way out? On bedrest, I cast
Robinson Crusoe
with the town's people
down to the goats, or someone
did. You say you said you want
to know me—

If I heard, I wasn't listening.
Know this: You are my person.
What you see is what you get:
An appetite

for emptiness. My skin
is a damp sheet
pulled over a drowned girl.
If not ovaries, then—? Too many
here to fit the vase.

I'm at the age
when nothing
becomes a playmate.
Thumbhole tapering to blade,
blade opening to finger hole—
I want to be a daisy

sliding stem-first
into a rifle's muzzle—a portrait
of war. My hand makes
a beak the steel imitates.
Two parts, two players.
One point
of pivot.

Song of the Lobe-Finned Fish

Goodbye to the bile green sea grass,
the creatures wreathed in poison tentacles,
the living aspic, half-congealed.
Will I miss that distant relative whose mouth
doubles as an anus, the one whose heart
beats through transparent skin, the unseen
legions bunched in holes and mounds,
the suckers and wanderers, producers of parchment
garlands, the makers of noxious ink,
of slime, the lurkers, posers, and hangers-on? No.
Nor the toothed, segmented, and hinged.
I'll yearn for the splayed introspective few
who thrive at great depths, their internal eyes
trained on spectacular truths—the ones
who never took the least interest in me.

Embolism

The oranges had taken two years to ripen on a tiny potted tree. My friend and her husband picked and peeled them. "We appreciated them," he says, and I imagine how they ate the wedges, feeding some to their dog, Julie, who would have wagged her tail, prone to express any small joy.

I think of the oranges ripening synchronous with the clot, not so much through a system of secret signals as a mutual achievement—the blood's lazy spooling and the fruit's sweetening—of themselves, the way a chorus of bullfrogs coincides with the appearance of robber flies in June.

Waking

A raven perches at the top of a lodgepole pine,
his oily iridescence undone by a low bank of cloud.

He croaks—four repetitions of the same note
and then four more.

We walk and listen to his guttural call.
He carries on, alone on a spare branch, until

a muffled response comes, like thought
to memory. The near raven waits silent,

his black beak closed on the certainty of the other.
You push the carriage. The baby sleeps.

The smell of smoke from distant forests burning,
trees hurled downstream in the thaw

—snagged and loosed and snagged again,
wasting in their slow trajectory—

churn under the current of her dreams.
We wheel along, knowing there's no promise

she'll live above horror or outlast us.
When she surfaces from sleep, we sing.

Notes:

On the Epigraphs:

    Bessie Head's quote is from her short prose piece "My Home," in *The Cardinals* (Heinemann, 1993), p. 124.

    The second quote is from Clarice Lispector, *A Breath of Life (Pulsations)* (New Directions, 2019), p. 71.

"Step Inside" (sections 4 and 5):

    Juan Valverde de Amusco, Andreas Vesalius and Gaspar Becerra were 16th century European anatomical illustrators. The historical information is condensed from the following biographical note on Valverde de Amusco's life and work in *Historical Anatomies on the Web*, a web database provided by the National Library of Medicine of the National Institutes of Health.

> Valverde's most famous work was *Historia de la composicion del cuerpo humano*, first published in Spanish in Rome, 1556. All but four of its 42 engraved copperplate illustrations were taken almost directly from Andreas Vesalius' *De humani corporis fabrica*. Vesalius bitterly commented on Valverde's plagiarism, accusing him of having performed very few dissections himself. Occasionally, however, Valverde corrected Vesalius' images, as in his depictions of the muscles of the eyes, nose, and larynx. One of Valverde's most striking original plates is that of a muscle figure holding his own skin in one hand and a knife in the other, which has been likened to Michelangelo's Saint Bartholomew in the Last Judgment section of the Sistine Chapel.
>
> The original illustrations were most likely drawn by Gaspar Becerra (1520?–1568?), a contemporary of Michelangelo, and the copperplate engravings are thought to have been carried out by Nicolas Beatrizet (1507?–1570?), whose initials "NB" appear on several of the plates.

"In the Garden of Intelligence":

    Information for the title and epigraph are from David Hancocks, *A Different Nature: The Paradoxical World of Zoos and Their Uncertain Future* (University of California Press, 2001), p. 8 and Vernon N. Kisling, ed., *Zoo and Aquarium History: Ancient Animal Collections to Zoological Gardens* (CRC Press, 2001), pp. 16-17.

    Pizarnik (1): "…the wild dog / isn't" is an iteration of Clarice Lispector's "The tulip is a tulip only in Holland. A lone tulip simply isn't." Clarice Lispector, *The Stream of Life* (University of Minnesota Press, 1989), p. 47.

Hikmet: "I didn't know I loved…" is borrowed from Nâzim Hikmet's poem "Things I Didn't Know I Loved." "[T]he little thing between the legs" comes from Hikmet's "Trousers and Skirts in Our Time." See Randy Blasing and Mutlu Konuk's translation, *Poems of Nazim Hikmet* (Persea Books, 1994) and Saime Göksu and Edward Timms, *Romantic Communist: The Life and Work of Nazim Hikmet* (St. Martin's Press, 1999).

Arbus: "Magic Piano" is mentioned as a form of "behavioral enrichment" used by zoos in David Grazian, *American Zoo: A Sociological Safari* (Princeton University Press, 2015), p. 27.

Pizarnik (2): "Jote, sos mi/ infatigable vos." *Jote* is a buzzard or vulture in Argentina, where Pizarnik is from. Here *vos* is a second person singular informal pronoun, "you." It's used for intimate address. *Vos* (you) and *voz* (voice), homophones in Latin American Spanish, are indistinguishable when spoken. Depending whether you saw the the text or heard it aloud, the translation could be taken to mean something like: "Buzzard, you're my tireless one" (as read) and "Buzzard, you're my unrelenting voice" (as heard).

Popa Whitman Popa: These lines are lifted directly from Vasko Popa and Walt Whitman: "Out of the blue womb of heaven," is found in "The Last Cord" in Vasko Popa, *Selected Poems* (Penguin, 1969), p. 89. "A shy and hidden bird is warbling a song" is from "When Lilacs Last in the Dooryard Bloom'd" in Whitman's *Drum-Taps: The Complete 1865 Edition* (NYRB/Poets, 2015), p. 102. "We mocked the song" is from "The Song of Young Truth" in the poem cycle "The Limetree in the Heart," Vasko Popa, *Collected Poems* (Anvil Press Poetry, 2011), p. 157.

Paglen: DARPA is the U.S. government's Defense Advanced Research Projects Agency.

Mayakovsky (2): Frank Morris and John and Clarence Anglin broke out of Alcatraz on June 12, 1962. It's not known if they survived their escape.

Full names of the artists and writers in this piece in order of appearance: Clarice Lispector, Alejandra Pizarnik, Nâzim Hikmet, Larry Levis, Italo Svevo, Sappho, John Baldessari, Philip Larkin, Diane Arbus, Audre Lorde, Christopher Smart, Gordon Matta-Clark, Henry "Box" Brown, Sor Juana Inés de la Cruz, Vladimir Mayakovsky, Vasko Popa, Walt Whitman, Trevor Paglen, Ovid, Janis Joplin

"Now":

Jan van Eyck was a Flemish painter (ca. 1390-1441) whose rendering of minute detail (pores in skin, individual hairs in a fur collar, wrinkle in an earlobe, pollen on a lily's stamen, etc.) and novel use of oil paint is said to have ushered in realism.

For a thoughtful discussion of Spanish explorer Álvar Núñez Cabeza de Vaca (1490-1559), see "The Blue of Distance" in Rebecca Solnit's *A Field Guide to Getting Lost* (Penguin Books, 2005), pp. 65-71.

"On Landmarks":

Definitions of landforms in italics are quoted from Robert Macfarlane's *Landmarks* (Penguin Random House UK, 2016), pp. 86-87.

"Jubilee":

The skeletal notation above the poem's title represents the chemical structure of paraquat dichloride (methyl viologen).

"The Poet and the Astronaut":

Armstrong's lines are quoted from National Aeronautics and Space Administration [NASA] (1969). *Apollo 8 onboard voice transcription* (Houston: Manned Spacecraft Center, retrieved from jsc. nasa.gov/history/mission_trans/AS08_CM.PDF).

"The Earth is blue like an orange" appears in Paul Éluard's poem by that title, translated by Mary Ann Caws in Mary Ann Caws, ed., *The Yale Anthology of Twentieth-Century French Poetry* (Yale University, 2004), p. 177. "…we have dreamt within us/ Space for the greatest silence" is from Éluard's "The Deaf and Blind," translated by Paul Auster in Paul Auster, ed., *The Random House Book of Twentieth-Century French Poetry* (Random House, 1982), p. 203. "The honeycomb of strength is stuffed with filth" is from "From the Depth of the Abyss," translated by Stephen Spender and Frances Cornford, found in the same volume (p. 219).

"If I Have One Regret—Send a Photo
So I Know How You Look—It's Not Having
Your Mother Committed :

In "Afterword," *ne plus ultra* (as defined by the OED) means "an impassible limit, obstacle or boundary;" "the peak of perfection" and "a command to go no further."

"Primes":

3: The apple mentioned is George Oppen's apple. See: Stephen Cope, ed. and George Oppen, *Selected Prose, Daybooks and Papers* (University of California Press, 2007), Day Book III, pp. 148-149. "With the word, we know it is the sea, we see the sea. *From outside it...* Without the word, we can feel as if from the inside. The taste of an apple, the sensation of sunlight—with the word, we see, *we see from the outside*."

59: All the musical equivalents to sounds were devised by Michael Lorant. Note: In C-4, the -4 indicates which octave the note is in. C-4 equals middle C.

61: Manolete, Manuel Laureano Rodríguez Sánchez, was one of Spain's most renowned bullfighters. Both he and a bull (named Islero) died at the end of a fight in Linares in August 1947, each killing the other. A *traje de luces* is the sequined "suit of lights" worn by the matador. The words quoted here are from *The Day Manolete Was Killed*, a black and white 16mm film directed by Dave Butler and Barnaby Conrad, based on Barnaby Conrad's book *The Death of Manolete* (Phoenix Books, 2007).

67: *Komm, süsser Tod*, by Johann Sebastian Bach, translates "Come, Sweet Death."

71: The mention of Ernesto, the exiled mother and the Neva are all drawn from Marguerite Duras, *Summer Rain* (Collier Books, 1992).

73: "The Suitors and the Little Iron Man" are retold from "The Griffin" in Jacob and Wilhelm Grimm, *Grimm's Household Tales*, Vol. II (G. Bell and Sons, Ltd., 1884), pp. 246-252.

"Sea of Crisis":
Refers to the lunar "sea" *Mare Crisium*.

"Lake of Forgetting":
Refers to the lunar "lake" *Lacus Oblivionis*.

"Annuals":
The line "I want to leave myself in order to see" is from Clarice Lispector's "That's Where I'm Going" in *Soulstorms* (New Directions, 1984), p. 146. Her sentence reads: "I leave myself in order to see." The same line also echoes a comment by Cézanne recorded by Joachim Gasquet in which Cézanne says, "I begin to separate myself from the landscape, to see it." See: Michael Doran, ed., *Conversations with Cézanne* (University of California Press, 2001), p. 114.

"Dress and Stuff Your Pig":

     "Dress and stuff your pig," "Fried Rusk," "Muffins," "Pickled Plums," "Onion Custard" and "one pint new milk, blood warm" are quoted from Malinda Russell, *Mrs. Malinda Russell, An Experienced Cook: A Domestic Cook Book: Containing a Careful Selection of Useful Receipts for the Kitchen* (T.O. Ward, at the "True Northerner" Office, 1866).

"Yes—Not at All":

     The title is derived from a sentence in one of Robert Frost's journals, Robert Faggen, ed., *The Notebooks of Robert Frost* (The Belknap Press of Harvard University Press, 2006), p. 306, notebook 24r. Frost writes, "Say yes to anything the patient says and then add 'not exactly' and finally 'not at all.'"

About the Author

Naomi Mulvihill was a Margaret Murphy endowed fellow at the Fine Arts Work Center in Provincetown, MA. Her chapbook, *We All Might Be* (Factory Hollow Press) was awarded the 2022 Tomaž Šalamun Prize Editor's Choice Selection. Her poems have appeared in the *Kenyon Review Online*, *New Orleans Review*, *Salamander*, *Cimarron*, *West Branch*, and others, and has been featured in *Verse Daily*. She received the Page Davidson Clayton Prize for "Poly-, Ambi-" as the best poem appearing in *Michigan Quarterly Review* by an emerging poet in 2022. She is a veteran bilingual teacher in the Boston Public Schools.

About The Word Works

Since its founding in 1974, The Word Works has steadily published volumes of contemporary poetry and presented public programs. Its imprints include the Washington Prize, the Tenth Gate Prize, the Hilary Tham Capital Collection, and International Editions.

Monthly, The Word Works offers free literary programs in its Café Muse series, which also presents two high school winners of the Jacklyn Potter Young Poets Competition. Word Works programs have included "In the Shadow of the Capitol," a symposium and archival project on the African American intellectual community in segregated Washington, D.C.; the Gunston Arts Center Poetry Series; the Poet Editor panel discussions at The Writer's Center; master class workshops; and writing retreats in Tuscany, Italy.

As a 501(c)3 organization, The Word Works has received awards from the National Endowment for the Arts, the National Endowment for the Humanities, the D.C. Commission on the Arts and Humanities, the Witter Bynner Foundation, Poets & Writers, The Writer's Center, Bell Atlantic, the David G. Taft Foundation, and others, including many generous private patrons.

An archive of artistic and administrative materials in the Washington Writing Archive is housed in the George Washington University Gelman Library. The Word Works is a member of the Community of Literary Magazines and Presses and its books are distributed by Small Press Distribution.

wordworksbooks.org

Washington Prize Winners

Nathalie Anderson, *Following Fred Astaire*, 1998

Michael Atkinson, *One Hundred Children Waiting for a Train*, 2001

Molly Bashaw, *The Whole Field Still Moving Inside It*, 2013

Carrie Bennett, *biography of water*, 2004

Peter Blair, *Last Heat*, 1999

John Bradley, *Love-in-Idleness: The Poetry of Roberto Zingarello*, 1989,
    2ND edition 2014

Christopher Bursk, *The Way Water Rubs Stone*, 1988

Richard Carr, *Ace*, 2008

Jamison Crabtree, *Rel[AM]ent*, 2014

Jessica Cuello, *Hunt*, 2016

Barbara Duffey, *Simple Machines*, 2015

B. K. Fischer, *St. Rage's Vault*, 2012

Linda Lee Harper, *Toward Desire*, 1995

Ann Rae Jonas, *A Diamond Is Hard But Not Tough*, 1997

Meg Kearney, *All Morning the Crows*, 2020

Annie Kim, *Eros, Unbroken*, 2019

Susan Lewis, *Zoom*, 2017

Frannie Lindsay, *Mayweed*, 2009

Richard Lyons, *Fleur Carnivore*, 2005

Elaine Magarrell, *Blameless Lives*, 1991

Fred Marchant, *Tipping Point*, 1993, 2ND edition 2013

Nils Michals, *Gembox*, 2018

Ron Mohring, *Survivable World*, 2003

Barbara Moore, *Farewell to the Body*, 1990

Naomi Mulvihill, *The Knife Thrower's Girl*, 2022

Brad Richard, *Motion Studies*, 2010

Jay Rogoff, *The Cutoff*, 1994

Prartho Sereno, *Call from Paris*, 2007, 2ND edition 2013

Enid Shomer, *Stalking the Florida Panther*, 1987

John Surowiecki, *The Hat City After Men Stopped Wearing Hats*, 2006

Sharon Suzuki-Martinez, *The Loneliest Whale Blues*, 2021

Miles Waggener, *Phoenix Suites*, 2002

Charlotte Warren, *Gandhi's Lap*, 2000

Mike White, *How to Make a Bird with Two Hands*, 2011

Nancy White, *Sun, Moon, Salt*, 1992, 2ND edition 2010

George Young, *Spinoza's Mouse*, 1996

CPSIA information can be obtained
at www.ICGtesting.com
Printed in the USA
JSHW021205070423
40065JS00003B/19

9 781944 585686